Cogg Hill Camping Equipment Company Practice Set

for use with

FUNDAMENTAL ACCOUNTING PRINCIPLES

Fifteenth Edition

Kermit D. Larson
University of Texas at Austin, Emeritus

John J. Wild
University of Wisconsin at Madison

Barbara Chiappetta
Nassau Community College

Prepared by
Leland Mansuetti
Sierra College

Irwin McGraw-Hill

Boston Burr Ridge, IL Dubuque, IA Madison, WI New York San Francisco St. Louis
Bangkok Bogotá Caracas Lisbon London Madrid
Mexico City Milan New Delhi Seoul Singapore Sydney Taipei Toronto

Irwin/McGraw-Hill

A Division of The McGraw-Hill Companies

Cogg Hill Camping Equipment Company Practice Set for use with
FUNDAMENTAL ACCOUNTING PRINCIPLES

1 2 3 4 5 6 7 8 9 0 MAZ/MAZ 9 3 2 1 0 9 8

ISBN 0-07-030742-3

http://www.mhhe.com

COGG HILL CAMPING EQUIPMENT COMPANY

A Business Papers Practice Set with Special Journals

This practice set may be used any time after Chapters 1-8 of the text have been covered. This practice set shows how certain special journals can be used for a merchandising and service company. Specific guidance is provided on how to do this. The transactions and accounting records used in this practice set involve you, the student, in all phases of the accounting cycle, from journalizing transactions to closing the books. In this practice set, you are in the role of the bookkeeper. It involves the use of business papers rather than a listing of the transactions to give you a feeling for keeping the actual set of books. This practice set is structured around a manual system to permit your maximum participation. Details have been kept to a minimum by summarizing certain repetitious transactions into totals covering a number of days or the entire month. The estimated completion time is twelve to sixteen hours.

INTRODUCTION

The Cogg Hill company sells and rents camping equipment in Denver, Colorado. It is a sole proprietorship and is owned and operated by Samuel Stephens. The company sells camping equipment and outdoor clothing. The company also rents large tents and groups of assorted camping equipment (e.g., Types A, B, and C) to trail guides for camping trips. The terms of all sales and all rentals are "net 30." The company delivers the equipment to many of its customers. Others pick it up at the store. Mr. Stephens makes all deposits. He removes the cash from the cash register and lists all checks received on a deposit slip. He then gives the duplicate deposit slip to you for recording. The company's ledgers and journals include:

Journals	**Ledgers**
Sales Journal	General Ledger
Purchases Journal	Accounts Receivable Subsidiary Ledger
Cash Receipts Journal	Accounts Payable Subsidiary Ledger
Cash Disbursements Journal	
General Journal	

The accounting files include:

Name of File	**Business Papers to be Filed**
Sales and Rental Invoices	Bookkeeper's copy of sales invoices Bookkeeper's copy of rental invoices
Purchase Invoices	Purchase invoices and credit memoranda
Interoffice Memoranda	Interoffice memoranda received from Mr. Stephens
Checks to be signed	Checks prepared for Mr. Stephens'
Duplicate Deposit Slips	Bookkeeper's copy of deposit slips

The post-closing trial balance of the Cogg Hill Camping Equipment Company, as of May 31, was as follows:

Cash	$ 23,750.00	
Accounts Receivable	7,959.00	
Allowance for Doubtful Accounts		$ 280.00
Interest Receivable	28.00	
Notes Receivable – Cobb Corp. (6 month, 8 percent, due August 15)	4,200.00	
Merchandise Inventory	176,400.00	
Office Supplies	590.00	
Store Supplies	540.00	
Prepaid Insurance	900.00	
Office Equipment	17,250.00	
Accumulated Depreciation – Office Equipment		5,300.00
Store Equipment	69,500.00	
Accumulated Depreciation – Store Equipment		19,000.00
Camping Rental Equipment	162,450.00	
Accumulated Depreciation – Camping Rental Equipment		88,700.00
Building	350,000.00	
Accumulated Depreciation – Building		120,000.00
Accounts Payable		16,950.00
Mortgage Note Payable – 9%		160,000.00
Samuel Stephens, Capital		403,337.00
	$ 813,567.00	$ 813,567.00

Accounts Receivable Subsidiary Ledger

P. Davis	$	1,560
K. Gragg		1,274
H. Holmes		2,500
S. Peeples		1,525
A. Smith		800
J. Still		300
	$	7,959

Accounts Payable Subsidiary Ledger

Brooks Brothers	$	0
Drex Co.		2,100
Dixon Co.		4,250
Fulton, Inc.		0
Robinson Co.		3,215
Samson Dist.		500
Technical Corp.		4,125
Zappo Corp.		2,760
	$	16,950

INSTRUCTIONS

1. Examine the business papers that follow. They consist of sales invoices, rental invoices, purchase invoices, duplicate deposit slips, a credit memorandum, and interoffice memoranda. They appear in the order in which they come to the bookkeeper's attention. The actions you as bookkeeper should take regarding these are:

   a. Sales Invoices—Enter the information in the Sales Journal. Post to the Subsidiary Accounts Receivable Ledger. Then file the invoice in the Sales and Rental Invoices file.

   b. Rental Invoices—Enter the information in the Sales Journal. Post to the Subsidiary Accounts Receivable Ledger. Then file the invoice in the Sales and Rental Invoices file.

   c. Purchase Invoices—Enter the information in the Purchases Journal on the date the invoice is received for each purchase of merchandise inventory or supplies. Post to the Subsidiary Accounts Payable Ledger. Then file the invoice in the Purchases Invoice file. Mr. Stephens will tell you when to make payment on these invoices by sending you an interoffice memorandum.

   d. Credit Memorandum—Enter the information in the General Journal. Then file the memorandum with the related purchase invoice in the Purchase Invoices file.

   e. Duplicate Deposit Slips—You should write the amount of the deposit in the checkbook provided. Then you should record the information in the Cash Receipts Journal. All cash deposited is from cash sales of camping equipment and should be recorded as a credit to Sales. The checks listed are payments on account and should be recorded as credits to Accounts Receivable and posted to the Subsidiary Accounts Receivable Ledger. After you have recorded the deposit, file the deposit slip in the Duplicate Deposit Slips file.

   f. Interoffice Memoranda—The owner sends information to you, the bookkeeper, instructing you to do certain things such as prepare checks for his signature, establish a new account, and reclassify a previously recorded purchase. After you have taken the appropriate action, file the memorandum in the Interoffice Memorandum file. When Mr. Stephens asks you to prepare checks for his signature, the actions you should take are as follows:

Checks to be prepared—You should write the check in the checkbook provided. Then you should record the information in the Cash Disbursements Journal and file the check in the Checks to be Signed file. You are not authorized to sign checks and should not do so.

2. Remember to post daily the following:
   a. All transactions you record in the General Journal.
   b. Amounts from the Accounts Receivable debit column in the Sales Journal to each individual customer's account in the Subsidiary Accounts Receivable Ledger.
   c. Amounts from the Accounts Payable credit column in the Purchases Journal to each individual creditor's account in the Subsidiary Accounts Payable Ledger.
   d. Amounts from the Accounts Receivable credit column in the Cash Receipts Journal to each individual customer's account in the Subsidiary Accounts Receivable Ledger.
   e. Amounts from the Accounts Payable debit column in the Cash Disbursements Journal to each individual creditor's account in the Subsidiary Accounts Payable Ledger.

   Instructions for work to be performed at the end of the accounting period (of one month) appear below:

3. At the end of the month you should:
   a. Foot the special journals and post to the General Ledger.
   b. Prepare schedules for Accounts Receivable and Accounts Payable as of June 30, from the subsidiary ledgers and compare these totals to the control account balances in the General Ledger.
   c. Compare the balance shown in the checkbook with the Cash account balance.
   d. Prepare a Bank Reconciliation as of June 30, 19XX.
   e. Prepare the trial balance in the Trial Balance columns of the work sheet provided.
   f. Complete the work sheet after making the following adjusting entries:
      1. Prepare the necessary journal entries to adjust the Cash account (based on the bank reconciliation).
      2. Accrue the interest on the Cobb note for June.
      3. Record one month's depreciation on the following assets: building, $1,475; office equipment, $1,150; store equipment, $3,650; and camping rental equipment, $2,687.
      4. Adjust for possible uncollectible accounts assuming the estimated expense is .5 percent of the total of net credit sales and rentals.
      5. Record the expiration of $250 of prepaid insurance.
      6. Make entries based on the balance of the supplies on hand:
         a. office supplies, $944.55
         b. store supplies, $324.75
      7. Accrue salaries for 3 working days at $162.50 per day.
      8. Accrue interest payable on the mortgage for one month.
      9. Merchandise inventory on June 30, 19XX was $174,985.00.

You should now take appropriate action based on the business papers that follow the Chart of General Ledger Accounts.

CHART OF GENERAL LEDGER ACCOUNTS

Account	Account Number
Cash	101
Petty Cash	102
Accounts Receivable	106
Allowance for Doubtful Accounts	107
Interest Receivable	109
Notes Receivable	111
Merchandise Inventory	119
Office Supplies	124
Store Supplies	125
Prepaid Insurance	128
Office Equipment	163
Accumulated Depreciation—Office Equipment	164
Store Equipment	165
Accumulated Depreciation—Store Equipment	166
Camping Rental Equipment	167
Accumulated Depreciation—Camping Rental Equipment	168
Building	173
Accumulated Depreciation—Building	174
Accounts Payable	201
Interest Payable	203
Salaries Payable	209
Mortgage Note Payable – 9%	251
Samuel Stephens, Capital	301
Samuel Stephens, Withdrawals	302
Camping Equipment Rental Revenue	406
Interest Earned	409
Camping Equipment Sales	413
Purchases	505
Purchase Returns and Allowances	506
Purchase Discounts	507
Transportation-in	508
Depreciation Expense—Building	606
Depreciation Expense—Office Equipment	612
Depreciation Expense—Store Equipment	613
Depreciation Expense—Camping Rental Equipment	615
Salaries Expense	622
Interest Expense	633
Insurance Expense	637
Office Supplies Expense	650
Store Supplies Expense	651
Bad Debts Expense	656
Telephone Expense	688
Utilities Expense	690
Income Summary	901

BUSINESS PAPERS

Business Paper No. 1

COLORADO BANK

Member F.D.I.C.

Cogg Hill Camping Equipment Co.
Industrial Boulevard
Denver, Colorado 77787

June 3, , **19** XX

Coin			
Currency			
Checks	K. Gragg	1,274	00
Total		1,274	00

000156|| 1334567840| 09787

Business Paper No. 2

Inter-Office Memo	**From** Samuel Stephens	**Date** June 3, 19XX
To Bookkeeper	**Subject** Petty Cash Fund	

Establish a petty cash fund in the amount of $100.00 and issue the check to me.

Business Paper No. 3

Inter-Office Memo	**From** Samuel Stephens	**Date** June 4, 19XX
To Bookkeeper	**Subject** Cash Disbursements	

Please prepare a check to Zappo for $2,060 as partial payment on account.

Business Paper No. 4

Invoice # 47183

Purchase Invoice
ZAPPO!

Date June 2, 19XX

Sold to:
Cogg Hill Camping Equipment
Industrial Blvd.
Denver, Colorado, 77787

Customer Order No.	Our Order No.	Date Delivered	Delivered Via	Terms
6-1		6/2/19XX	Brown Trucking	2/10,n/60

Quantity ordered	Quantity shipped	Description	Unit Price	Amount
12	12	#37 Tents	255.00	3,060.00
23	23	#A-3 Sleeping Bags	70.50	1,621.50
18	18	#919 Canteens w/cover	18.00	324.00
		RECEIVED JUNE 5		
		Total		5,005.50

Customer's Copy

Business Paper No. 5

Invoice # R142-17

Rental Invoice
COGG HILL

Date June 5, 19XX

Rented to:
Mr. A. Smith
1073 Broad Road
Rocky Springs, Colorado, 76660

Length of Rental: ______ day(s)
1 week(s)

Customer Order No.	Our Order No.	Date Delivered	Delivered Via	Terms
127-99		6/7/19XX	Our truck	n/30

Quantity ordered	Quantity shipped	Description	Unit Price	Amount
3	3	Large Tents	135.00	405.00
12	12	Type A group of camping equipment	62.00	744.00
		Total		1,149.00

Bookkeeper's Copy

Business Paper No. 6

Invoice # R142-18

Rental Invoice
COGG HILL

Date June 5, 19XX

Rented to:
Ms. J. Still
2231 After Place
St. James, Colorado, 75127

Length of Rental: ______ day(s)
1 week(s)

Customer Order No.	Our Order No.	Date Delivered	Delivered Via	Terms
A-72		6/5/19XX	Customer picked up	n/30

Quantity ordered	Quantity shipped	Description	Unit Price	Amount
12	12	Type B group of camping equipment	265.00	3,180.00
		Total		3,180.00

Bookkeeper's Copy

Business Paper No. 7

Invoice # S323-02

Sales Invoice
COGG HILL

Date June 5, 19XX

Sold to:
Ms. J. Still
2231 After Place
St. James, Colorado, 75127

Customer Order No.	Our Order No.	Date Delivered	Delivered Via	Terms
A-12		6/5/19XX	Customer pick up	n/30

Quantity ordered	Quantity shipped	Description	Unit Price	Amount
30	30	Sleeping Bags	88.95	2,668.50
		Total		2,668.50

Bookkeeper's Copy

Business Paper No. 8

Invoice # 842

Purchase Invoice
Samson Distributors

Date June 4, 19XX

Sold to:
Cogg Hill Camping Equipment
Industrial Blvd.
Denver, Colorado, 77787

Customer Order No.	Our Order No.	Date Shipped	Delivered Via	Terms
6-2		6/4/19XX	Eastland Trucking	2/10,n/60

Quantity ordered	Quantity shipped	Description	Unit Price	Amount
1	1	Large Tent V-135	725.35	725.35
		RECEIVED JUNE 8 Total		725.35

Business Paper No. 9

Invoice # 0047983

Purchase Invoice
Brooks Brothers

Date June 7, 19XX

Sold to:
Cogg Hill Camping Equipment
Industrial Blvd.
Denver, Colorado, 77787

Customer Order No.	Our Order No.	Date Shipped	Shipped Via	Terms
6-7		6/7/19XX	Our Truck	2/10,n/60

Quantity ordered	Quantity shipped	Description	Unit Price	Amount
14	14	Down Jackets #1378 S/4. M/5, L/5	144.35	2,020.90
		assorted colors		0.00
8	8	Rain Ponchos #435 – one size fits all	38.15	305.20
8	8	Hiking Boots #171-m Assorted sizes	71.25	570.00
		Total		2,896.10
		RECEIVED JUNE 8		

Business Paper No. 10

Invoice # S323-03

Sales Invoice
COGG HILL

Date June 9, 19XX

Sold to:
Mr. S. Peeples
46 Cady Road
St. James, Colorado, 75127

Customer Order No.	Our Order No.	Date Delivered	Delivered Via	Terms
39		6/9/19XX	Customer picked up	n/30

Quantity ordered	Quantity shipped	Description	Unit Price	Amount
5	5	Down Jackets	296.00	1,480.00
3	3	Tents	525.00	1,575.00
3	3	Hammocks	100.00	300.00
		Total		3,355.00

Bookkeeper's Copy

Business Paper No. 11

Inter-Office Memo	**From** Samuel Stephens	**Date** June 9, 19XX
To Bookkeeper	**Subject** Reclassification of Merchandise	

Please transfer the large tent purchased from Samson Distributors (Invoice #842, Received June 8) from the Purchases account to the Camping Rental Equipment account. This tent will be used for rental purposes, not resale.

Business Paper No. 12

COLORADO BANK

Member F.D.I.C.

Cogg Hill Camping Equipment Co.
Industrial Boulevard
Denver, Colorado 77787

June 9, , **19** XX

Coin		2	30
Currency		3,100	00
Checks	H. Holmes	2,500	00
Total		5,602	30

000156||1334567840|. 09787

Business Paper No. 13

Inter-Office Memo	**From** Samuel Stephens	**Date** June 9, 19XX
To Bookkeeper	**Subject** Cash Disbursements	

Please prepare check to Zappo Corp. for the payment of the following invoices:

Invoice	46504	4/15	$ 700.00
Invoice	47183	6/2	$ 5,005.50

Business Paper No. 14

Invoice # S323-04

Sales Invoice
COGG HILL

Date June 10, 19XX

Sold to:
Mr. P. Davis
22 Evers Avenue
St. James, Colorado, 75127

Customer Order No.	Our Order No.	Date Delivered	Delivered Via	Terms
V-707		6/10/19XX	Customer picked up	n/30

Quantity ordered	Quantity shipped	Description	Unit Price	Amount
10	10	Hiking Boots	137.95	1,379.50
10	10	Rain Ponchos	75.15	751.50
		Total		2,131.00

Bookkeeper's Copy

Business Paper No. 15

Inter-Office Memo	From Samuel Stephens	Date June 11, 19XX
To Bookkeeper	Subject Cash Disbursements	

Please prepare check to Dex Corporation for payment in full of account balance.

Business Paper No. 16

COLORADO BANK

Member F.D.I.C.

Cogg Hill Camping Equipment Co.
Industrial Boulevard
Denver, Colorado 77787

June 12, , **19** XX

Coin			
Currency			
Checks	A. Smith	800	00
	P. Davis	1,560	00
Total		2,360	00

Business Paper No. 17

Inter-Office Memo	**From** Samuel Stephens	**Date** June 12, 19XX
To Bookkeeper	**Subject** Cash Disbursements	

Please prepare your payroll check. Salary for the period ending June 12 is $1,625.

Business Paper No. 18

Invoice # R142-19

Rental Invoice
COGG HILL

Date June 13, 19XX

Rented to:
Ms. K. Gragg
P.O. Box 27
Reed City, Colorado 75155

Length of Rental ______ day(s)
1 week(s)

Customer Order No.	Our Order No.	Date Delivered	Delivered Via	Terms
100		6/13/19x	Customer picked up	n/30

Quantity ordered	Quantity shipped	Description	Unit Price	Amount
11	11	Type B group of camping equipment	265.00	2,915.00
		Total		2,915.00

Bookkeeper's Copy

Business Paper No. 19

Invoice # S323-05

Sales Invoice
COGG HILL

Date June 13, 19XX

Sold to:
Mr. K. Gragg
P.O. Box 27
Reed City, Colorado, 75166

Customer Order No.	Our Order No.	Date Delivered	Delivered Via	Terms
100		6/13/19XX	Customer Picked up	n/30

Quantity ordered	Quantity shipped	Description	Unit Price	Amount
7	7	Ground Cloth	24.45	171.15
1	1	2-burner Stove	86.25	86.25
		Total		257.40

Bookkeeper's Copy

Business Paper No. 20

Inter-Office Memo	From: Samuel Stephens	Date: June 14, 19XX
To: Bookkeeper	**Subject:** Cash Disbursements	

Please prepare check for Robinson Co. for $2,315.

Business Paper No. 25

Invoice # R142-20

Rental Invoice
COGG HILL

Date June 17, 19XX

Rented to:
Mr. H. Holmes
Box 32 Utah Road
St. James, Colorado 75127

Length of Rental 6 day(s)
week(s)

Customer Order No.	Our Order No.	Date Delivered	Delivered Via	Terms
Phone Order		6/19/19XX	Our Truck	n/30

Quantity ordered	Quantity shipped	Description	Unit Price	Amount
8	8	Type C group of camping equipment	212.00	1,696.00
		Total		1,696.00

Bookkeeper's Copy

Business Paper No. 26

Inter-Office Memo	**From** Samuel Stephens	**Date** June 19, 19XX
To Bookkeeper	**Subject** Cash Disbursements	

Prepare check to Central Colorad Electric Company for utilities in the amount of $725.45.

Business Paper No. 27

COLORADO BANK

Member F.D.I.C.

Cogg Hill Camping Equipment Co.
Industrial Boulevard
Denver, Colorado 77787

June 19, **, 19** XX

Coin		18	45
Currency		5,125	00
Checks	J. Still	1,750	00
Total		6,893	45

000156||1334567840| 09787

Business Paper No. 28

Invoice # 72876

Purchase Invoice
Dex Company

Date June 20, 19XX

Sold to:
Cogg Hill Camping Equipment
Industrial Blvd.
Denver, Colorado 77787

Customer Order No.	Our Order No.	Date Shipped	Shipped Via	Terms
6-6		6/20/19XX	Midway	2/10,n/60

Quantity ordered	Quantity shipped	Description	Unit Price	Amount
22	22	Nylon Rope	14 15	311 30
10	10	#3-P Air Mattresses	28 00	280 00
14	14	#XYZ Polyethylene Ground Cloth	13 10	183 40
16 sets	16	Plastic Tent Stakes	21 45	343 20
		RECEIVED JUNE 22		
		Total		1,117 90

Business Paper No. 29

Invoice # S323-07

Sales Invoice
COGG HILL

Date June 23, 19XX

Sold to:
Mr. S. Peeples
46 Cady Road
St. James, Colorado, 75127

Customer Order No.	Our Order No.	Date Delivered	Delivered Via	Terms
41		6/23/19XX	Customer picked up	n/30

Quantity ordered	Quantity shipped	Description	Unit Price	Amount
8	8	2-burner Stoves	86.25	690.00
		Total		690.00

Bookkeeper's Copy

Business Paper No. 30

Inter-Office Memo	**From** Samuel Stephens	**Date** June 25, 19XX
To Bookkeeper	**Subject** Cash Disbursements	

Please prepare checks to:

Dixon Co. for payment in full on account.

Technical Corp. for $2,125 as a partial payment on camping equipment.

Business Paper No. 31

Invoice # S323-08

Sales Invoice
COGG HILL

Date June 25, 19XX

Sold to:
Ms. J. Still
2231 After Place
St. James, Colorado, 75127

Customer Order No.	**Our Order No.**	**Date Delivered**	**Delivered Via**	**Terms**
A-73		6/25/19XX	Customer picked up	n/30

Quantity ordered	**Quantity shipped**	**Description**	**Unit Price**	**Amount**
8	8	Cooking Kit	89.25	714.00
4	4	Canteens w/covers	32.95	131.80
		Total		845.80

Bookkeeper's Copy

Business Paper No. 32

Inter-Office Memo	**From** Samuel Stephens	**Date** June 26, 19XX
To Bookkeeper	**Subject** Cash Disbursements	

Prepare a check to N. Central Telephone for phone services of $345.30

Prepare your payroll check. Salary for the period ending June 27 is $1,625.

Business Paper No. 33

Invoice # S323-09

Sales Invoice
COGG HILL

Date June 26, 19XX

Sold to:
Mr. A. Smith
1073 Broad Street
Rocky Springs, Colorado, 76660

Customer Order No.	Our Order No.	Date Delivered	Delivered Via	Terms
128-00		6/29/19XX	Our truck	n/30

Quantity ordered	Quantity shipped	Description	Unit Price	Amount
2	2	1-burner Stove	63 45	126 90
		Total		126 90

Bookkeeper's Copy

Business Paper No. 34

COLORADO BANK

Member F.D.I.C.

Cogg Hill Camping Equipment Co.
Industrial Boulevard
Denver, Colorado 77787

June 26, , **19** XX

Coin		15	50
Currency		3,875	00
Checks	S. Peeples	1,525	00
Total		5,415	50

0001 56||1334567840| 09787

Business Paper No. 35

Inter-Office Memo	**From** Samuel Stephens	**Date** June 26, 19XX
To Bookkeeper	**Subject** Cash Disbursements	

Please prepare a check to Brooks Brothers for payment in full on account.

Business Paper No. 36

Invoice # 9764

Purchase Invoice
Samson Distributors

Date June 25, 19XX

Sold to:
Cogg Hill Camping Equipment
Industrial Blvd.
Denver, Colorado 77787

Customer Order No.	Our Order No.	Date Shipped	Shipped Via	Terms
6-8		6/2/19XX	Brown	2/10,n/60

Quantity ordered	Quantity shipped	Description	Unit Price	Amount
5	5	Igloo Ice Chest - 4 gallon	25.00	125.00
12	12	Igloo Thermos; 1 gal.	11.00	132.00
3	3	Grills - #120	16.25	48.75
6	6	Sierra Cooking Kits – Small	36.95	221.70
6	6	Emergency Medical Kits – Standard	32.90	197.40
		RECEIVED JUNE 29	Total	724.85

Business Paper No. 37

Invoice # 42730

Purchase Invoice
DIXON Company

Date June 27, 19XX

Sold to:
Cogg Hill Camping Equipment
Industrial Blvd.
Denver, Colorado 77787

Customer Order No.	Our Order No.	Date Shipped	Shipped Via	Terms
6-9		6/27/19XX	Ballard Truck	2/10,n/60

Quantity ordered	Quantity shipped	Description	Unit Price	Amount
4	4	Shovel - back pack	23.30	93.20
12	12	Knife - Alaskan	16.10	193.20
12	3	Hatchets - back pack	21.00	63.00
6	6	Back Packs - Large	32.00	192.00
6	6	Hammock - canvas	46.00	276.00
		RECEIVED JUNE 29 Total		817.40

Business Paper No. 38

COLORADO BANK

Member F.D.I.C.

Cogg Hill Camping Equipment Co.
Industrial Boulevard
Denver, Colorado 77787

June 30, , **19** XX

Coin		7	25
Currency		4,156	00
Checks	J. Still	2,148	50
	S. Peeples	3,355	00
Total		9,666	75

000156||1334567840|.09787

Business Paper No. 39

Inter-Office Memo	**From** Samuel Stephens	**Date** June 30, 19XX
To Bookkeeper	**Subject** Note Receivable	

Please record a 60-day, 7% note receivable from K. Gragg dated June 30 in settlement of account receivable.

Business Paper No. 40

Inter-Office Memo	**From** Samuel Stephens	**Date** June 30, 19XX
To Bookkeeper	**Subject** Draw	

Please issue check to me for $6,000.00

Business Paper No. 41

Inter-Office Memo	**From** Samuel Stephens	**Date** June 30, 19XX
To Bookkeeper	**Subject** Petty Cash	

Please issue a check to me for $97.87 to replenish the petty cash fund. Paid receipts and petty cash vouchers are attached for the following:

Petty Cash Vouchers	For	
No. 1	Transportation-In	$32.00
No. 2	Transportation-In	36.95
No. 3	Transportation-In	28.92

COGG HILL CAMPING EQUIPMENT COMPANY

Bank Reconciliation

May 31, 19XX

Balance per ledger, May 31, 19XX				$ 23,750.00
Balance per bank statement, May 31, 19XX				25,692.55
Less: Outstanding checks				
No. 414			$ 550.00	
No. 415			87.55	
No. 417			1,305.00	1,942.55
Adjusted Cash Balance, May 31, 19XX				$ 23,750.00

Colorado Bank

1145 Armory Place
Denver, Colorado 77781

Cogg Hill Camping Equipment Company
Industrial Blvd.
Denver, Colorado 77787

Statement Date June 30, 19XX
Business Checking Account

Balance last Statement	Deposits	Checks and Debits	Service Charge	Balance this Statement
25,692.55	21,545.25	26,057.39	-	21,180.41

Date		Checks and Other Debits			Deposits
June	3	100.00	550.00		1,274.00
	4	2,060.00			
	9	5,605.39	87.55		5,602.30
	11	2,100.00			
	12	1,625.00	1,305.00		2,360.00
	14	2,315.00			
	19	725.45			6,893.45
	25	4,084.00			
	25	2,125.00	1,750.00	NSF	
	26	1,625.00			5,415.50

JOURNALS

SALES JOURNAL

Date	Customer	Invoice No.	PR	A/R Dr. Sales Cr.	A/R Dr. Rental Revenue Cr.

PURCHASES JOURNAL

Date	Account	Date of Invoice	Terms	PR	Acct. Pay Cr.	Purchases Dr.	Office Supplies Dr.	Other Accounts Dr.

Date	Account Credited	Explanation	PR	Cash Debit	Amounts Receivable Credit	Sales Credit

CASH DISBURSEMENTS JOURNAL

Date	Chk. No.	Payee	Account Debited	PR	Cash Credit	Purchase Discount Credit	Other Accounts Debit	Accounts Payable Debit

Date		Account Titles and Explanation	Post Ref.	Debit			Credit		

GENERAL JOURNAL

Date		Account Titles and Explanation	Post Ref.	Debit			Credit		

Date	Account Titles and Explanation	Post Ref.	Debit	Credit

GENERAL JOURNAL

Page 57

Date	Account Titles and Explanation	Post Ref.	Debit	Credit

Date	Account Titles and Explanation	Post Ref.	Debit	Credit

GENERAL LEDGER AND ACCOUNTS RECEIVABLE AND ACCOUNTS PAYABLE SUBSIDIARY LEDGERS

General Ledger

Cash — **Account No. 101**

DATE		EXPLANATION	POST REF.	DEBIT	CREDIT	BALANCE
May	31	Balance				23,750.00

Petty Cash — **Account No. 102**

DATE		EXPLANATION	POST REF.	DEBIT	CREDIT	BALANCE

Accounts Receivable — **Account No. 106**

DATE		EXPLANATION	POST REF.	DEBIT	CREDIT	BALANCE
May	31	Balance				7,959.00

Allowance for Doubtful Accounts — **Account No. 107**

DATE		EXPLANATION	POST REF.	DEBIT	CREDIT	BALANCE
May	31	Balance				280.00

Interest Receivable — **Account No. 109**

DATE		EXPLANATION	POST REF.	DEBIT	CREDIT	BALANCE
May	31	Balance				28.00

Notes Receivable — Account No. 111

DATE		EXPLANATION	POST REF.	DEBIT	CREDIT	BALANCE
May	31	Cobb Corp. Note				4 200 00

Merchandise Inventory — Account No. 119

DATE		EXPLANATION	POST REF.	DEBIT	CREDIT	BALANCE
May	31	Balance				176 400 00

Office Supplies — Account No. 124

DATE		EXPLANATION	POST REF.	DEBIT	CREDIT	BALANCE
May	31	Balance				590 00

Store Supplies — Account No. 125

DATE		EXPLANATION	POST REF.	DEBIT	CREDIT	BALANCE
May	31	Balance				540 00

Prepaid Insurance — Account No. 128

DATE		EXPLANATION	POST REF.	DEBIT	CREDIT	BALANCE
May	31	Balance				900 00

Office Equipment — Account No. 163

DATE		EXPLANATION	POST REF.	DEBIT	CREDIT	BALANCE
May	31	Balance				17 250 00

Accumulated Depreciation—Office Equipment Account No. 164

DATE		EXPLANATION	POST REF.	DEBIT	CREDIT	BALANCE
May	31	Balance				5 300 00

Store Equipment Account No. 165

DATE		EXPLANATION	POST REF.	DEBIT	CREDIT	BALANCE
May	31	Balance				69 500 00

Accumulated Depreciation—Store Equipment Account No. 166

DATE		EXPLANATION	POST REF.	DEBIT	CREDIT	BALANCE
May	31	Balance				19 000 00

Camping Rental Equipment Account No. 167

DATE		EXPLANATION	POST REF.	DEBIT	CREDIT	BALANCE
May	31	Balance				162 450 00

Accumulated Depreciation—Camping Rental Equipment Account No. 168

DATE		EXPLANATION	POST REF.	DEBIT	CREDIT	BALANCE
May	31	Balance				88 700 00

Building Account No. 173

DATE		EXPLANATION	POST REF.	DEBIT	CREDIT	BALANCE
May	31	Balance				350 000 00

Accumulated Depreciation—Building — Account No. 174

DATE		EXPLANATION	POST REF.	DEBIT	CREDIT	BALANCE
May	31	Balance				120,000.00

Accounts Payable — Account No. 201

DATE		EXPLANATION	POST REF.	DEBIT	CREDIT	BALANCE
May	31	Balance				16,950.00

Interest Payable — Account No. 203

DATE		EXPLANATION	POST REF.	DEBIT	CREDIT	BALANCE
May	31	Balance				0.00

Salaries Payable — Account No. 209

DATE		EXPLANATION	POST REF.	DEBIT	CREDIT	BALANCE
May	31	Balance				0.00

Mortgage Note Payable—9% — Account No. 251

DATE		EXPLANATION	POST REF.	DEBIT	CREDIT	BALANCE
May	31	Balance				160,000.00

Samuel Stephens, Capital — Account No. 301

DATE		EXPLANATION	POST REF.	DEBIT	CREDIT	BALANCE
May	31	Balance				403,337.00

Samuel Stephens, Withdrawals — **Account No. 302**

DATE		EXPLANATION	POST REF.	DEBIT	CREDIT	BALANCE

Camping Equipment Rental Revenue — **Account No. 406**

DATE		EXPLANATION	POST REF.	DEBIT	CREDIT	BALANCE

Interest Earned — **Account No. 409**

DATE		EXPLANATION	POST REF.	DEBIT	CREDIT	BALANCE

Camping Equipment Sales — **Account No. 413**

DATE		EXPLANATION	POST REF.	DEBIT	CREDIT	BALANCE

Purchases — **Account No. 505**

DATE		EXPLANATION	POST REF.	DEBIT	CREDIT	BALANCE

Purchase Returns and Allowances — **Account No. 506**

DATE		EXPLANATION	POST REF.	DEBIT	CREDIT	BALANCE

Purchases Discounts Account No. 507

DATE		EXPLANATION	POST REF.	DEBIT	CREDIT	BALANCE

Transportation—In Account No. 508

DATE		EXPLANATION	POST REF.	DEBIT	CREDIT	BALANCE

Depreciation Expense—Building Account No. 606

DATE		EXPLANATION	POST REF.	DEBIT	CREDIT	BALANCE

Depreciation Expense—Office Equipment Account No. 612

DATE		EXPLANATION	POST REF.	DEBIT	CREDIT	BALANCE

Depreciation Expense—Store Equipment Account No. 613

DATE		EXPLANATION	POST REF.	DEBIT	CREDIT	BALANCE

Depreciation Expense—Camping Rental Equipment Account No. 615

DATE		EXPLANATION	POST REF.	DEBIT	CREDIT	BALANCE

Salaries Expense Account No. 622

DATE		EXPLANATION	POST REF.	DEBIT	CREDIT	BALANCE

Interest Expense Account No. 633

DATE		EXPLANATION	POST REF.	DEBIT	CREDIT	BALANCE

Insurance Expense Account No. 637

DATE		EXPLANATION	POST REF.	DEBIT	CREDIT	BALANCE

Office Supplies Expense Account No. 650

DATE		EXPLANATION	POST REF.	DEBIT	CREDIT	BALANCE

Store Supplies Expense Account No. 651

DATE		EXPLANATION	POST REF.	DEBIT	CREDIT	BALANCE

Bad Debts Expense Account No. 656

DATE		EXPLANATION	POST REF.	DEBIT	CREDIT	BALANCE

Telephone Expense **Account No. 688**

DATE	EXPLANATION	POST REF.	DEBIT	CREDIT	BALANCE

Utilities Expense **Account No. 690**

DATE	EXPLANATION	POST REF.	DEBIT	CREDIT	BALANCE

Income Summary **Account No. 901**

DATE	EXPLANATION	POST REF.	DEBIT	CREDIT	BALANCE

Accounts Receivable
Subsidiary Ledger

P. Davis 22 Evers Avenue St. James, Colorado 75127

DATE		EXPLANATION	POST REF.	DEBIT	CREDIT	BALANCE
May	31	Balance				1 560 00

K. Gragg P.O. Box 27 Reed City, Colorado 75166

DATE		EXPLANATION	POST REF.	DEBIT	CREDIT	BALANCE
May	31	Balance				1 274 00

H. Holmes Box 32 Utah Road St. James, Colorado 75127

DATE		EXPLANATION	POST REF.	DEBIT	CREDIT	BALANCE
May	31	Balance				2 500 00

S. Peeples 46 Cady Road St. James, Colorado 75127

DATE		EXPLANATION	POST REF.	DEBIT	CREDIT	BALANCE
May	31	Balance				1 525 00

A. Smith 1073 Broad Road Rocky Springs, Colorado 76660

DATE		EXPLANATION	POST REF.	DEBIT	CREDIT	BALANCE
May	31	Balance				800 00

J. Still 2231 After Place St. James, Colorado 75127

DATE		EXPLANATION	POST REF.	DEBIT	CREDIT	BALANCE
May	31	Balance				300 00

Accounts Payable
Subsidiary Ledger

Brooks Brothers **P.O. Box 2970** **St. James, Colorado 75127**

DATE		EXPLANATION	POST REF.	DEBIT	CREDIT	BALANCE
May	31	Balance				0

Dex Company **1711 Nevada Avenue** **Boulder, Colorado 75555**

DATE		EXPLANATION	POST REF.	DEBIT	CREDIT	BALANCE
May	31	Balance				2 100 00

Dixon Company **3783 Company Road** **Smith's Peak, Utah 83000**

DATE		EXPLANATION	POST REF.	DEBIT	CREDIT	BALANCE
May	31	Balance				4 250 00

Fulton, Inc. **Route #4** **Colorado Springs, Colorado 74140**

DATE		EXPLANATION	POST REF.	DEBIT	CREDIT	BALANCE
May	31	Balance				0

Robinson Company **31 Industrial Blvd.** **St. James, Colorado 75127**

DATE		EXPLANATION	POST REF.	DEBIT	CREDIT	BALANCE
May	31	Balance				3 215 00

Samson Distributors 1938 Danck Street Castletown, Nevada 95177

DATE		EXPLANATION	POST REF.	DEBIT	CREDIT	BALANCE
May	31	Balance				500 00

Technical Corporation 1010 33rd Street Rocky Springs, Colorado 76660

DATE		EXPLANATION	POST REF.	DEBIT	CREDIT	BALANCE
May	31	Balance				4 125 00

Zappo Corporation 577 Snow Street Valleybrook, Montana 81111

DATE		EXPLANATION	POST REF.	DEBIT	CREDIT	BALANCE
May	31	Balance				2 760 00

SCHEDULES, FINANCIAL STATEMENTS, WORK SHEET, AND POST-CLOSING TRIAL BALANCE

COGG HILL CAMPING EQUIPMENT COMPANY

Schedule of Accounts Receivable

June 30, 19XX

COGG HILL CAMPING EQUIPMENT COMPANY

Schedule of Accounts Payable

June 30, 19XX

COGG HILL CAMPING EQUIPMENT COMPANY

Bank Reconciliation

June 30, 19XX

	ACCOUNT TITLES	TRIAL BALANCE		ADJUSTMENTS	
		DR.	CR.	DR.	CR.

EQUIPMENT COMPANY

Ended June 30, 19XX

ADJUSTED TRIAL BALANCE		INCOME STATEMENT		BALANCE SHEET	
DR.	CR.	DR.	CR.	DR.	CR.

COGG HILL CAMPING

Work Sheet for Month

	ACCOUNT TITLES	TRIAL BALANCE		ADJUSTMENTS	
		DR.	CR.	DR.	CR.

EQUIPMENT COMPANY

Ended June 30, 19XX

ADJUSTED TRIAL BALANCE		INCOME STATEMENT		BALANCE SHEET	
DR.	CR.	DR.	CR.	DR.	CR.

COGG HILL CAMPING EQUIPMENT COMPANY

Income Statement

For the Month Ended June 30, 19XX

COGG HILL CAMPING EQUIPMENT COMPANY

Statement of Owner's Equity

For the Month Ended June 30, 19XX

COGG HILL CAMPING EQUIPMENT COMPANY

Balance Sheet

June 30, 19XX

COGG HILL CAMPING EQUIPMENT COMPANY

Post-Closing Trial Balance

June 30, 19XX

No. 418 $ ______

______ 19______

PAY TO ______

FOR

	DOLLARS	CENTS
BAL BRO'T FOR'D		
(ADD DEPOSITS OR SUBRACT ANY CHARGES		
NEW BALANCE		
AM'T THIS CHECK		
BAL CAR'D FOR'D		

Cogg Hill Camping Equipment Company **418**

______ 19___ 64-10/610

PAY TO THE ORDER OF ______ $ ______

______ DOLLARS

COLORADO BANK

FOR ______ ______

Accounting Practice Set

No. 419 $ ______

______ 19______

PAY TO ______

FOR

	DOLLARS	CENTS
BAL BRO'T FOR'D		
(ADD DEPOSITS OR SUBRACT ANY CHARGES		
NEW BALANCE		
AM'T THIS CHECK		
BAL CAR'D FOR'D		

Cogg Hill Camping Equipment Company **419**

______ 19___ 64-10/610

PAY TO THE ORDER OF ______ $ ______

______ DOLLARS

COLORADO BANK

FOR ______ ______

Accounting Practice Set

No. 420 $ ______

______ 19______

PAY TO ______

FOR

	DOLLARS	CENTS
BAL BRO'T FOR'D		
(ADD DEPOSITS OR SUBRACT ANY CHARGES		
NEW BALANCE		
AM'T THIS CHECK		
BAL CAR'D FOR'D		

Cogg Hill Camping Equipment Company **420**

______ 19___ 64-10/610

PAY TO THE ORDER OF ______ $ ______

______ DOLLARS

COLORADO BANK

FOR ______ ______

Accounting Practice Set

No. 421 $ ______

______ 19______

PAY TO ______

FOR

	DOLLARS	CENTS
BAL BRO'T FOR'D		
(ADD DEPOSITS OR SUBRACT ANY CHARGES		
NEW BALANCE		
AM'T THIS CHECK		
BAL CAR'D FOR'D		

Cogg Hill Camping Equipment Company **421**

______ 19___ 64-10/610

PAY TO THE ORDER OF ______ $ ______

______ DOLLARS

COLORADO BANK

FOR ______ ______

Accounting Practice Set

No. 422 $ ______

______________ 19______

PAY TO ______________

FOR

	DOLLARS	CENTS
BAL BRO'T FOR'D		
(ADD DEPOSITS OR SUBRACT ANY CHARGES		
NEW BALANCE		
AM'T THIS CHECK		
BAL CAR'D FOR'D		

Cogg Hill Camping Equipment Company **422**

______________ 19___ 64-10/610

PAY TO THE ORDER OF ______________ $ ______

______________________________ DOLLARS

COLORADO BANK

FOR ______________ ______________

Accounting Practice Set

No. 423 $ ______

______________ 19______

PAY TO ______________

FOR

	DOLLARS	CENTS
BAL BRO'T FOR'D		
(ADD DEPOSITS OR SUBRACT ANY CHARGES		
NEW BALANCE		
AM'T THIS CHECK		
BAL CAR'D FOR'D		

Cogg Hill Camping Equipment Company **423**

______________ 19___ 64-10/610

PAY TO THE ORDER OF ______________ $ ______

______________________________ DOLLARS

COLORADO BANK

FOR ______________ ______________

Accounting Practice Set

No. 424 $ ______

______________ 19______

PAY TO ______________

FOR

	DOLLARS	CENTS
BAL BRO'T FOR'D		
(ADD DEPOSITS OR SUBRACT ANY CHARGES		
NEW BALANCE		
AM'T THIS CHECK		
BAL CAR'D FOR'D		

Cogg Hill Camping Equipment Company **424**

______________ 19___ 64-10/610

PAY TO THE ORDER OF ______________ $ ______

______________________________ DOLLARS

COLORADO BANK

FOR ______________ ______________

Accounting Practice Set

No. 425 $ ______

______________ 19______

PAY TO ______________

FOR

	DOLLARS	CENTS
BAL BRO'T FOR'D		
(ADD DEPOSITS OR SUBRACT ANY CHARGES		
NEW BALANCE		
AM'T THIS CHECK		
BAL CAR'D FOR'D		

Cogg Hill Camping Equipment Company **425**

______________ 19___ 64-10/610

PAY TO THE ORDER OF ______________ $ ______

______________________________ DOLLARS

COLORADO BANK

FOR ______________ ______________

Accounting Practice Set

No. 426 $ ______

______ 19______

PAY TO ______

FOR

	DOLLARS	CENTS
BAL BRO'T FOR'D		
(ADD DEPOSITS OR SUBRACT ANY CHARGES		
NEW BALANCE		
AM'T THIS CHECK		
BAL CAR'D FOR'D		

Cogg Hill Camping Equipment Company **426**

______ 19___ 64-10/610

PAY TO THE ORDER OF ______ $ ______

______ DOLLARS

COLORADO BANK

FOR ______ ______

Accounting Practice Set

No. 427 $ ______

______ 19______

PAY TO ______

FOR

	DOLLARS	CENTS
BAL BRO'T FOR'D		
(ADD DEPOSITS OR SUBRACT ANY CHARGES		
NEW BALANCE		
AM'T THIS CHECK		
BAL CAR'D FOR'D		

Cogg Hill Camping Equipment Company **427**

______ 19___ 64-10/610

PAY TO THE ORDER OF ______ $ ______

______ DOLLARS

COLORADO BANK

FOR ______ ______

Accounting Practice Set

No. 428 $ ______

______ 19______

PAY TO ______

FOR

	DOLLARS	CENTS
BAL BRO'T FOR'D		
(ADD DEPOSITS OR SUBRACT ANY CHARGES		
NEW BALANCE		
AM'T THIS CHECK		
BAL CAR'D FOR'D		

Cogg Hill Camping Equipment Company **428**

______ 19___ 64-10/610

PAY TO THE ORDER OF ______ $ ______

______ DOLLARS

COLORADO BANK

FOR ______ ______

Accounting Practice Set

No. 429 $ ______

______ 19______

PAY TO ______

FOR

	DOLLARS	CENTS
BAL BRO'T FOR'D		
(ADD DEPOSITS OR SUBRACT ANY CHARGES		
NEW BALANCE		
AM'T THIS CHECK		
BAL CAR'D FOR'D		

Cogg Hill Camping Equipment Company **429**

______ 19___ 64-10/610

PAY TO THE ORDER OF ______ $ ______

______ DOLLARS

COLORADO BANK

FOR ______ ______

Accounting Practice Set

No. 430 $

19

PAY TO

FOR

	DOLLARS	CENTS
BAL BRO'T FOR'D		
(ADD DEPOSITS OR SUBRACT ANY CHARGES		
NEW BALANCE		
AM'T THIS CHECK		
BAL CAR'D FOR'D		

Cogg Hill Camping Equipment Company **430**

19 64-10/610

PAY TO THE ORDER OF $

DOLLARS

COLORADO BANK

FOR

Accounting Practice Set

No. 431 $

19

PAY TO

FOR

	DOLLARS	CENTS
BAL BRO'T FOR'D		
(ADD DEPOSITS OR SUBRACT ANY CHARGES		
NEW BALANCE		
AM'T THIS CHECK		
BAL CAR'D FOR'D		

Cogg Hill Camping Equipment Company **431**

19 64-10/610

PAY TO THE ORDER OF $

DOLLARS

COLORADO BANK

FOR

Accounting Practice Set

No. 432 $

19

PAY TO

FOR

	DOLLARS	CENTS
BAL BRO'T FOR'D		
(ADD DEPOSITS OR SUBRACT ANY CHARGES		
NEW BALANCE		
AM'T THIS CHECK		
BAL CAR'D FOR'D		

Cogg Hill Camping Equipment Company **432**

19 64-10/610

PAY TO THE ORDER OF $

DOLLARS

COLORADO BANK

FOR

Accounting Practice Set

No. 433 $

19

PAY TO

FOR

	DOLLARS	CENTS
BAL BRO'T FOR'D		
(ADD DEPOSITS OR SUBRACT ANY CHARGES		
NEW BALANCE		
AM'T THIS CHECK		
BAL CAR'D FOR'D		

Cogg Hill Camping Equipment Company **433**

19 64-10/610

PAY TO THE ORDER OF $

DOLLARS

COLORADO BANK

FOR

Accounting Practice Set